BELOW COLD MOUNTAIN

Below Cold Mountain

JOSEPH STROUD

詩 COPPER CANYON PRESS

The publication of this book was supported by grants from the Lannan Foundation, the National Endowment for the Arts, and the Washington State Arts Commission, and by contributions from Elliott Bay Book Company, James Laughlin, and the members of the Friends of Copper Canyon Press. Copper Canyon Press is in residence with Centrum at Fort Worden State Park.

The quotation from Han-shan on page 3 is translated by Burton Watson in *Cold Mountain*, Columbia University Press (1970).

FRONTISPIECE ART: Lucas Cranach, *Cupid Complaining to Venus*. Reproduced by courtesy of the Trustees, The National Gallery, London.

COVER ART: Kenneth Callahan, *Mountain Landscape*. Ink on paper, 22¼ x 29½, Foster/White Gallery.

Library of Congress Cataloging-in-Publication Data

Stroud, Joseph, 1943–
Below Cold Mountain : poems / by Joseph Stroud.
p. cm.
ISBN 1-55659-084-9
I. Title.
PS3569.T73 B45 1998
811'.54 – ddc21   98-8919

COPPER CANYON PRESS
P.O. BOX 271, PORT TOWNSEND, WASHINGTON 98368

For Mike & Tim, Ellen & Sam, Charis & Rachel,
our lives together below Cold Mountain

&

To Han-shan, across the years,
who discovered the Mountain was inside him

CONTENTS

BELOW COLD MOUNTAIN

I climb the road to Cold Mountain,
The road to Cold Mountain that never ends.
The valleys are long and strewn with stones;
The streams broad and banked with thick grass.
Moss is slippery, though no rain has fallen;
Pines sigh, but it isn't the wind.
Who can break from the snares of the world
And sit with me among the white clouds?

— HAN-SHAN

Provenance

I want to tell you the story of that winter
in Madrid where I lived in a room
with no windows, where I lived
with the death of my father, carrying it
everywhere through the streets,
as if it were an object, a book written
in a luminous language I could not read.
Every day I left my room and wandered
across the great plazas of that city,
boulevards crowded with people and cars.
There was nowhere I wanted to go.
Sometimes I would come to myself
inside a cathedral under the vaulted
ceiling of the transept, I would find
myself sobbing, transfixed in the light
slanting through the rose window
scattering jewels across the cold
marble floor. At this distance now
the grief is not important, nor the sadness
I felt day after day wandering the maze
of medieval streets, wandering the rooms
of the Prado, going from painting
to painting, looking into Velázquez,
into Bosch, Brueghel, looking for something
that would help, that would frame
my spirit, focus sorrow into some
kind of belief that wasn't fantasy
or false, for I was tired of deception,
the lies of words, even the Gypsy violin,
its lament with the *puñal* inside
seemed indulgent, posturing.
I don't mean to say these didn't
move me, I was an easy mark,

anything could well up in me –
rainshine on the cobblestone streets,
a bowl of tripe soup in a peasant café.
In my world at that time there was
no scale, nothing with which
to measure, I could no longer
discern value – the mongrel eating
scraps of garbage in the alley
was equal to *Guernica* in all its
massive outrage. When I looked
in the paintings mostly what I saw
were questions. In the paradise
panel of *The Garden of Earthly Delights*
why does Bosch show a lion
disemboweling a deer? Or that man
in hell crucified on the strings of a harp?
In his *Allegory of the Seven Deadly Sins*:
Gluttony, Lust, Sloth, Wrath, Envy, Avarice,
Pride – of which am *I* most guilty?
Why in Juan de Flanders' *Resurrection
of Lazarus* is the face of Christ so sad
in bringing the body back to life?
Every day I returned to my room,
to my cave where I could not look out
at the world, where I was forced into
the one place I did not want to be. In
the Cranach painting – behind Venus
with her fantastic hat, her cryptic look,
behind Cupid holding a honeycomb, whimpering
with bee stings – far off in the background,
that cliff rising above the sea, that small hut
on top – is that Cold Mountain, is that where
the poet made his way out of our world?
My father had little use for poems, less use
for the future. If he had anything

to show me by his life, it was to live
here. Even in a room without windows.
One day in the Prado, in the Hall
of the Muses, a group of men
in expensive suits, severe looking,
men of importance, with a purpose,
moved down the hallway toward me,
and I was swept aside, politely,
firmly. As they passed I glimpsed
in their midst a woman, in a simple
black dress with pearls, serene, speaking
to no one, and then she and the men
were gone. *Who was that?* I asked,
and a guard answered: *The Queen.*
The Queen. In my attempt to follow
to see which painting she would choose,
I got lost in one of the Goya rooms
and found myself before one of his
dark paintings, one from his last years
when the world held no more illusions,
where love was examined in a ruthless,
savage anger. In this painting
a woman stood next to Death, her beauty,
her elegance, her pearls and shining hair
meant nothing in His presence,
and He was looking out from the painting,
looking into me, and Death took my hand
and made me look, and I saw my own face
streaming with tears, and the day
took on the shape of a crouching beast,
and my father's voice called out in wonder
or warning, and every moment
I held on made it that much harder
to let go, and Death demanded
that I let go. Then the moment

disappeared, like a pale horse, like
a ghost horse disappearing deep inside
Goya's painting. I left the Prado.
I walked by the *Palacio Real* with its
2,000 rooms, one for every kind
of desire. I came upon the *Rastro*,
the great open-air bazaar, a flea market
for the planet, where everything in the world
that has been cast aside, rejected, lost,
might be found, where I found Cervantes,
an old, dusty copy of *Don Quixote*,
and where I discovered an old mirror,
and looking into it found my father's face
in my face looking back at me,
and behind us a Brueghel world
crowded with the clamor of the market,
people busy with their lives, hunting,
searching for what's missing. How casual
they seemed, in no hurry, as if they had all
of time, no frenzy, no worry,
as the Castilian sun made its slow
arch over us, the same sun
that lanced the fish on crushed ice
in the market stalls, fish with open mouths,
glazed stares, lapped against each other
like scales, by the dozens, the *Madrileños*
gaping over them, reading them
like some sacred text, like some kind
of psalm or prophecy as they made
their choice, and had it wrapped in paper,
then disappeared into the crowd.
And that is all. I wanted to tell you
the story of that winter in Madrid
where I lived in a room with no windows
at the beginning of my life without my father.

When the fascist officials asked Picasso
about *Guernica*: "Are you responsible
for this painting?" He looked back
at them, and answered slowly: "No.
You are." What should I answer
when asked about this poem?
I wanted to tell you the story of that winter
in Madrid, where my father kept dying, again
and again, inside of me, and I kept
bringing him back, holding him for as long
as I could. I never knew how much
I loved him. I didn't know that grief
would give him back to me, over
and over, I didn't know that those
cobbled streets would someday
lead to here, to this quietude,
this blessing, to my father
within me.

I

*A Suite
for the Common*

The Magician

Across the ravine from the mill house there's a grassy patch
where Gypsies keep a donkey tied to a tree. Sometimes
I'll cross the stream and bring him an apple, holding it out
like a rare jewel. He'll contemplate it, then take my whole
hand into his lips as soft as suede, and I can't tell how he
does it, but when his head lifts back, the apple has disappeared.

Night in Day

The night never wants to end, to give itself over
to light. So it traps itself in things: obsidian, crows.
Even on summer solstice, the day of light's great
triumph, where fields of sunflowers guzzle in the sun –
we break open the watermelon and spit out
black seeds, bits of night glistening on the grass.

Homage to Rolf Jacobsen

The yellow jacket keeps crashing against the pane
trying to get out. All along it's only a matter
of opening the window, finding the words,
and you're out there – in the other, larger world.
To the dead, paradise is the sidewalk you stroll down
looking in windows, humming, stopping for coffee.

Homage to the Black Walnut
in Downtown Santa Cruz

Late afternoon, trudging from the bank to the bookstore,
I stop and look up at the black walnut on Cedar Street,
into its green canopy of leaves and immense curving limbs.
A tree is a place, not an object, it's an island in the air
where our sight may live awhile, unburdened
and free from this heavy, earthen body.

Mercy, Mercy

In Lombok I woke to what felt like the knick of razor blades
on my scalp. I grabbed a flashlight – and there on the pillow
where my head had been – a half-circle of cockroaches,
the color of burnt butter, sitting in full lotus, antennae
weaving mantras, on their faces the beatific smile
of Samantabhadra, the bodhisattva of merciful kindness.

That Life is a Circle of Heraclitean Fire

Not an original observation, but it's what I thought
when I saw lotus flowers floating on the surface of a pond
and the village girls were catching little flames of dragonflies
and stringing them around their waists and the emerald
on the lily pad changed to a frog that jumped and disappeared
into the black water out of which the jewel in the lotus blossoms

The First Law of Thermodynamics

He was a good ole boy, and when he died his friends carried out
his final wish – the body was cremated and the ashes stuffed
into shotgun shells. They walked through the woods he loved
and fired aimlessly into the trees – he came down everywhere
in a powdery rain, a pollen of ashes that once was the memory
of a boy walking under trees showering him with leaves.

Chaos Theory: Equation

The sun multiplied by bees equals honey and the addition
of leaves with rain is the sum of nights in summer
when pines ooze the resin time turns to amber
on the necklace around the throat of the woman
dividing her past by mornings in the spell of flowers
factored by the love marriage makes of yearning & desire

The Orchard

In the spring night the petals are luminous and look like stars,
each tree a pulsing, bright nebula. Summer, the limbs sag
with the weight of apples, *golden delicious* hanging like globes
of small suns, a fusion of sugar in their core. The windfall apples
are crushed and pulped into cider, the liquid a rich amber
the color of the moon rising slowly in the thick, autumn dusk.

All Through the Night the Mockingbird Sang

Of course there's no coffee, I forgot to buy some, and dammit,
Sam lost the key to the lock on his bike, I'll have to drive him
to school, I'm running late myself, the car's nearly out of gas,
I'll have to stop and fill it – auguries, omens of the day ahead
I'm thinking – when I begin to hear them, faint, rising up
inside me, those all-night songs, like dark honey, like psalms.

Every Summer the Riots

Late spring and the nasturtiums are behaving themselves, just poking
their leaves over the flower box. But I know it won't be long now –
this morning I noticed the first tentative shoot peering out
to where sunlight floods the garden, and I can see the jeweled heads
whispering in the leaves – soon they'll make a break for it, soon
the tendrils will bolt across the deck, swarming toward light.

Lost

The deer turns his head away from me and casually
continues along the ridge not even glancing back
to where I stand, to where I begin to walk across
a field of snow inside my body and lose myself
as a white ash drifts from the sky filling my tracks
and there is no way to find my way back.

Love in the Classical World

Suddenly there was Ellen's favorite hen shrieking
and rising into the air clutched in the single talon of a hawk.
Or the night the raccoon exploded out of the henhouse
with a hen in its mouth. How beautiful, how elegant,
how perfect the shape of an egg. Ellen gathers them
every morning, holds one above the skillet, breaks it open.

Biophysics

Photographs on the refrigerator held in place by magnets –
one of Sam, seven years ago, climbing out of the Grand Canyon.
The same boy who that summer caught his first cutthroat, stunned
by the iridescence of scales in sunlight. Who enters the house now
in the almost body of a man, jerks open the fridge door, and stares
hungrily – ravenous for *anything* in this world there is to eat.

Hear That Phone Ringing?
Sounds Like a Long Distance Call

Death is talking on the phone, long distance to somebody,
I'm outside the booth, waiting to call home, impatient,
trying not to be obvious about it, while Death yammers on,
now and then looking over in my direction, his empty gaze
not meant for me, I hope, as I think of that poor guy
on the other end, clutching his phone, not ready to hang up.

What She Told Me in Orland, California

My son's a sheriff. He'll find a dead possum on the road –
if it's male he'll cut the penis off – there's a little bone in there –
then he'll boil the meat off it, and stick this sharp penis bone
in his hatband. Uses it for a toothpick. I swear to you
it's a man's world. But if I'm ever reborn – a snake, a kangaroo –
whatever – it damn well better not have a penis along with it.

The Life of a Dog

Marie understands: *Go get your rug! Want to go for a ride?*
Time to eat! Where's your toy? BAD *dog!* GOOD *dog!*
But she has problems with *Come back here! Don't jump*
on the guest! At times when we're alone, when she's looking
pensive, I'll say to her slowly and sadly, *What do you think*
of existential angst? She'll look up and her tail will wag & wag.

Go Fetch It!

Intelligence in animals is often measured by their capacity
to amuse themselves when alone. In this they resemble
poets. We too know how to bury the bone and then return
surprised that we have found it. We have no tail to wag,
but when the Muse says *Bark!* – we bark. We roll over.
We're as happy as the dog who gets to ride in the car.

Matar la Noche

I'm in a taverna eating *tapas* and drinking a glass of wine
listening to Pepe tell me of the Spanish way: *Each moment
is to be savored. We drink to make the mind sparkle, not
to get drunk, like those Germans yesterday – two hours
and the night was finished for them. They're very good
at making money, but we can teach them how to spend it.*

The Nightingales of Andalucía

He begins to tell me about the nightingales singing in the ravine:
– Oh yeah, they're there. You see, the female's on one side
and the male's on the other, and she says, *Look, you silly bastard,
get over here and fix this nest. If you think I'm going to lay eggs in it,
you're nuts.* And he says, *Can't right now, Honey.* And she says,
Well then, fuck off. That's what the nightingales are singing. –

And I Raised My Hand in Return

Every morning for two weeks on my walk into the village
I would see the young goat on the grassy slope above the stream.
It belonged to the Gypsies who lived in the plaza below the castle.
One day on my walk back to the mill house I saw the little goat
hanging from a tree by its hind legs, and a Gypsy was pulling
the skin off with a pair of pliers which he waved to me in greeting.

Hacedor

After a lifetime of leaning over his guitar,
Segovia offered this aesthetic of craft: *Not more,
not less.* When approaching the romance of spirit,
Put on the brakes. Too much music, isn't music.
Be calm. Let the word do its work. Allow
each string its resonance in silence.

He Asked, and We Began the Train into the Heart

I settled into the compartment. It would be three days from Benares
to Madras. The Hindu across from me smiled, but we didn't speak.
Everyone, everything I knew, was on the other side of the planet.
I had no life I could call my own, no miracles, no cure. 100 miles
into the oldest, most worn-out landscape I had ever seen, the man
clapped his hands softly together – *And so, shall we speak of love?*

My Father Died

I put down the phone. I put down the phone.
What is there to hold onto? Now grief
will have its way. There is a great machine
in the blackness that dismantles one moment
from the next. It makes the sound of the heart
but is heartless.

The Others, O Lord, For My Time
Has Not Yet Come

In a room of the Prado many people stop to gaze
at Brueghel's *The Triumph of Death*, a window
into the nightmare of plague – a great battlefield
where Death's legions begin the massacres.
Like everyone, I search for myself among the living,
the ones fleeing, among those trying to escape the canvas.

I Was Not Prepared for the Death of My Father

On the plains of La Mancha I met Don Quixote. I wanted
to tell him I was fleeing my father's death. In the train to Toledo,
into the light of El Greco, in the rain falling over the Tagus,
in the olive, the cathedral, I had fled. And finally into Cervantes –
I would join Sancho, I too would serve the knight, and ride
to Montiel. *Someone, please. Close the book. Leave me there.*

In the Maze Garden of the *Generalife*

In the Arab quarter below the Gypsy caves of Sacramonte,
Lorca heard a lament flashing like a blade – the *cante jondo*
of Andalucía where *death drifts in and out the tavern*
with the keel of the moon. Grief is a true labyrinth. I enter
the maze on the Hill of the Sun, threading the memory
of my father through each day of the years to come.

He Told Me to Come Back and See

I returned to the farmhouse where twenty years ago I watched
as Pete ground a walnut into the earth with his boot.
He smiled at me then, as if he knew some important secret.
And sure enough, in that spot there's now a large walnut tree.
Pete's been dead ten years. Back then I knew little about love,
of choices, or the great limbs that live inside the seed.

Love's More Difficult Translation

About five years into the marriage
he thought his heart had finally translated it.
But it was like that night at the Foreign Film Festival
halfway through a movie when suddenly
it switched from subtitles to dubbed English
& for an instant he thought he understood Romanian.

The Song of Divorce

Bitter the warmth of sunlight, and bitter the taste of apple,
the song and the stars and wheat fields, bitter the memory,
moonlight, the shine of the lake's surface in morning
like a sheen of pearl, bitter the hummingbird's throat
and gold pollen, all poems and their music, harp wood
and sandalwood, *bitter,* silk sheets, fire, the marriage.

In This Flesh

The bluebottle fly lit next to the scratch on my arm
and with its probing tongue began to sip at the blood –
what Hamlet would call a *reechy kiss*. I brushed it away
into its brief world stewed in corruption where the sun breeds
maggots in a dead dog. *No more marriages,* Hamlet told Ophelia.
No more honeying and making love over the nasty sty.

Where Language Fails

It's a parade coming down the street and everyone gathers
on the sidewalk to watch – troubadour poets, W. B. Yeats,
even Mandelstam's there looking a bit wild-eyed. The band's
playing *Alexander's Ragtime Band*. This is the way it is when
I'm with you. *Love* isn't the word for it. Here comes the man
with the cymbals – where they *clash* is how you live in me.

In Puerto Vallarta Once

And then we're in her room and she's unbuttoning her blouse –
we're both wrecked – sunlight shouts on the bed – dazzling –
and she begins to take off her earrings, miniature skeletons
that do a little jig as her fingers unclasp them – she wants me
to take her – *Look at me, I'm wet* – and then she crouches
and puts her mouth against the buckle of my belt –

Reading Cavafy Alone in Bed

I, too, remember the past, my room lit by candles,
and the night she entered and touched my face
with her face, with mouth and tongue and lips,
in the orchard night, in the odor of fruit,
her breasts – remember, body? – that room,
remember? – our cries, the flickering candles?

Idle

The *perezoso*, slow bear, what we call the sloth,
who hangs from limbs upside down and never moves
for days, its long fur dangling with moss, and when
at last it turns its slow head to peer at you, you've already
given away everything you own, you've planted yourself,
arms becoming limbs, your spirit unsheathing in leaves.

Come and Get It

So little. So much. Seasons. The orchard snowing
with blossoms. Night fall and day break. Systole.
Diastole. The path leads into the woods to the house
where the old woman invites you in to admire her oven.
Don't go! we plead – we who have been cooked
and eaten, we who sit here gripping our forks and knives.

In the Body of the Dragon

Hawthorne thought the human heart was a chamber
and if you devised the key to open it you might find
a dragon. Or an angel. Those who see the latter
walk in summer fields comforted by the blazing
chaos of sun, bees writhing in the throats of flowers,
fingers and lips stained with the blood of blackberries.

And for This Also I am Ashamed

Dawn, and I have to catch a bus on the outskirts of Pondicherry.
So I hire a trishaw. In the darkness I don't notice at first
the man suffers from elephantiasis, his legs huge and heavy.
He pedals so slowly we're never going to make it on time and I
shout at him to hurry as we pass the glowing coals of cigarettes
that lepers balance carefully on the stumps of their hands.

After the Opera

Coming out of the theater surrounded by people
in elegant clothes, jewelry, all the arias finished, no one
able to hold the music inside for long, soon enough
it's gone, and it's night in the city, it's all neon and noise,
the woman you're with stops to adjust her shoe, leans
her body against yours for a moment, balancing.

From Time to Time
Turning My Head to See

In the washed-out arroyo through the old part of town,
below the level of the streets, & full of trash, broken bottles,
I saw one day while driving the road to Tomatlán
the huge head and bulk of a bull elephant standing
in a pool next to the burned-out wreck of a car and a woman
over and over whipping clothes against an enormous boulder.

Die Schwermut

In Trakl it's always evening and autumn, blue silence,
the dark shapes of shepherds, angels, a lunar voice
of the sister, and the final gold of fallen stars. It is world's
end, a synæsthesia of childhood and melancholy, a vision
that could not manage the agony of the wounded soldier
who put a pistol to his head and pulled the trigger.

The Words of Chilam Balam

On the first night of the world's last days the foreigners come.
The quetzal sings no more, the jaguar flees, the deer are headless,
trees hang with the fruit of corpses, no priests can read the signs.
Gone the great wheel with its rose on whose petals are inscribed
the book of years – now these strangers with beards and pale eyes.
Prepare now for whips and fire and blood and sorrow and sorrow.

Babette

This is where they lived, Babette and her family, all of them
gone now, Babette with her red hair and freckles, tormented
by the boys in second grade, Babette who never made it
into history, whose life mattered only to a few, Babette,
a brief incarnation, who grew into a woman, then vanished
from my life, and from yours, O my sisters and brothers.

Missing

I keep looking for my face to appear on a milk carton,
a photo of little me, missing since '52 or '53, who left home
without saying goodbye, left his brothers playing baseball,
left his parents glancing up from breakfast, wondering at this
solitary son who sets out every morning, and returns slightly
more lost, each time less of the child he left home with.

Earth Angel

We were like children. It made little difference
who we were dancing with, just holding a girl close
for the first time and shuffling to the music was enough
in our strange new bodies, listening to the lyrics
of heartbreak and yearning – it was like paradise –
walking home with my twin, neither of us speaking.

Can You Hear It?

What is the sound the spirit makes when the body
walks across the plaza of a white village in Andalucía,
when the mind gazes out across the rooftops of Siena
among the swallows and the many shades of dusk?
The dog rises suddenly out of sleep, cocks its head,
gazes toward the door, listening to the other side.

The Years
Like Crows Coming Home to Roost

Outside my window a single crow over the grove
forty years ago and when I look again there are legions
winging into the trees, their shapes like sable embers
flaming into black tongues, squalling among themselves
in the raucous unspeakable syllables of some primal,
alien world, cawing down the night to cover them.

Waking on the Shining Path

Riding the night bus to Ayacucho, jouncing,
lurching into sleep, dreamless, and then suddenly
waking, like dropping off a cliff, the bus stopped,
a village square somewhere, the driver is shouting
at a man who's waving a pistol, outside the window
ghost limbs of trees fluorescent in the streetlamp.

In Sepia

She would comb her hair sitting on the edge of the bed
in her nightgown – long, pure strokes, again and again,
pulling through snarls until the hair sheened with light –
Watching her, her calm face, arms raising, lifting her breasts,
I can remember thinking, believing – *So this is the happiness
I've come to – this is my life – this, too, is what I live for.*

This Waiting

All morning I've been watching a bee among the trumpet vines
thrumming from one bud to another, brushing against them
as if desire alone would make them bloom. All morning
I've been waiting for the poem to appear as it did for Rumi
when he beheld Shams of Tabriz, the Beloved, and words
opened like daybreak, like chords of fire within his body.

Love Like a Catch of Fire

I think of Lady Izumi's poem mourning the death of Atsumichi,
how consoled she would be if only she could see his face
once more, even for a moment, as in a flash of lightning – *Seen
Unseen*. One thousand years ago, and love has not changed.
I never saw the oriole in the green leaves, just a flash of gold.
Do you think the morning won't come when you'll wake alone?

These Nights, Passing Through

Between us and death are all the days and nights
from which we fashion our life. Don't bother
to count them. They won't add up to enough.
All evening I've been listening to Netania Davrath
singing songs from the Auvergne, the music
quieting in me, the way stars dissolve in the dawn.

Dissolving

Standing above the ghats, looking down on the river,
the bodies burning, my own thoughts burning,
remembering the silk merchant in the chowk
unrolling a bolt of cobalt fire over the floor,
pouring chai into a clay cup, smiling, offering me
a nugget of sugar to place under my tongue.

No Lexicon

When I arrived, the table had already been set – plates
from China, crystal, silverware, two burning candles.
From the kitchen the aroma of basmati, cumin, ginger.
She stood in the doorway. A summer evening. A feast.
To that moment I brought everything I had, and what
I had we have no word for, though some call it *hunger*.

Ezra Under the Constellation of the Dragon

And what shall I raise against my righteousness,
what put down anger, take from the root of my heart
vanity? I have wept and I have raved in the temple
the cottonwood makes of leaves, knelt down within
the day, death's other kingdom, and still the earth
would have of me, & the night come down in points of fire.

Comice

I think of Issa often these days, his poems about the loneliness
of fleas, watermelons becoming frogs to escape from thieves.
Moon in solstice, snowfall under the earth, I dream of a pure life.
Issa said of his child, *She smooths the wrinkles from my heart.*
Yes, it's a dewdrop world. Inside the pear there's a paradise
we will never know, our only hint the sweetness of its taste.

Rock Me on the Waters

Whitman says, *All has been gentle with me.* Lucky him.
Lucky the one who has no account with lamentation.
And yet of it we string the harp for a larger music.
The sun pours down honey over the bodies of lovers
who make of their bed a small boat that rocks in the sea
of morning, rocking in waves, of light and leavings.

Our Blood is Red Coral, We Build a Bridge Over the Abyss

I don't know if Kazantzakis ever walked the mountains of
     Kárpathos.
Or visited the village of Ólimbos that looks down on the Aegean.
Above the pines are the orchards of stone and light. No one lives
     there.
But one day while walking, I heard a music – bagpipe and small bells
followed by a shepherd with his goats – up there, in midsummer,
in the furnace of the sun, in that place even the gods have
     abandoned.

Simple Gifts

The sun makes sugar in the melon, gathers sweetness
in us, builds a tower of joy in the paradise we call *body*.
Everywhere I look I see voices – the loquat's pale
gold fruit, the cottonwood's leaves, sprays of lilac.
Even the mockingbird high in the walnut tree listens
to the loud bees as if within a honeycomb of music.

And the White Goat Tethered to a Fig Tree Above the Blue Aegean

If it happens that I am to go down into the underworld –
let no one say I went willingly, without regret or tears,
if even to see Eurydice with my own eyes among the shades
or to pitch my tent in that dark world of memory and desire
and listen to Dante sing of Beatrice. Say how I struggled
leaving this world of sunlight and strawberries and night stars

2

Homages

/

Voices

Homage to Life

(*Jules Supervielle*, HOMMAGE À LA VIE)

It is good to have chosen
a living home
and harbored time
in a constant heart,
to have seen one's hands
touch the world
as an apple
in a small garden,
to have loved the earth,
the moon and the sun,
like old friends
beyond any others,
and to have entrusted
the world to memory
like a luminous horseman
to his black steed,
to have given shape
to these words: wife, children,
and to have served as a shore
for roving continents,
to have come upon the soul
with little oarstrokes
for it is frightened
by a sudden approach.
It is good to have known
the shade under the leaves
and to have felt age
steal over the naked body
accompanying the grief
of dark blood in our veins
and glazing its silence

with the star, Patience,
and to have all these words
stirring in the head,
to choose the least beautiful
and make a little feast for them,
to have felt life
rushed and ill-loved,
to have held it
in this poetry.

Listening to Leon

My time's coming, and that's a hard thing to say, I go to bed at
     night not certain I'll be here in the morning, I got this fear lying
     in the dark, I can't sleep and I'm scared of thinking

Every afternoon loud music from the neighbor's place, she calls it
     rap, rhymes with *crap*, but everyone's got their own music,
     it's been years since I heard *Body and Soul*, never thought I'd
     hear anything better, and I haven't, Coleman Hawkins, 1939,
     Memphis, a juke joint, drinking whiskey, twenty-five years old,
     my whole body filled with music, a couple of years before the
     War

I don't know, I don't know, that's what I say, not I don't care or
     I don't think so, it's not a negative thing, no, it's not some loose
     change you get from every mother's son, I don't know, you
     know what I mean?

I miss the woman, the mornings mostly, the sweetness like a ripe
     peach, all those years reaching my hand into the leaves, feeling
     around in there for the touch, and I never knew when the last
     one was the last one

Thirty-two years I drove a bus, watched coins drop, people paying
     to get from here to there, thirty-two years to get here, retired
     they call it, but I'm not tired, I'm just old, like everybody else
     I buy my onions and carrots at the market, I don't own
     property, when I was a boy I planted some seeds, squash and
     bush beans, sweet corn, in the Georgia summer, a simple thing,
     a garden, some dirt and water, some sun, some time

Walking home after the dance, you know what I mean, a bit weary but feeling good, still hearing the music, remembering how we danced, walking out of town, into the country, a big night sky with stars, the music faint, but holding onto it, remembering, humming, sometimes that's the way it is for me

Islands

You all time malicious, mon
askin the questions
no answer
I got

What it be
you lookin sad sad?
De woman she
got you money?

Jes keep on, mon
This road be
where you be
gon to

If you ain listen
to the sea
by now
you ain never
hear it

The light from behind
the sun
make this day on the island
great day

Even the he goat
be still

❧

Dat fish he for you, mon
From de bottom
all de way up
he eye
on you

❧

You look
at de mango
long long
like it gon
talk

❧

Aw mon
dat walk be you trouble
De rum shop be where
I see you from
you come
on de way
back

❧

No
dat de part
you *doan*
eat

❧

I bring it
up
she take it
down
so *she*
say

❧

I been en these goddom islands
me whole fucken life
an I no cryin
bout it
yet

❧

Yah mon
from way back
en de mountain
de mot mot
he make
he song

Autumn

(*from the Man'yōshū*)

So
it comes to this –
And we thought our love
would last a thousand years

(*Ōtomo no Yakamochi*)

※

Last night you sent me away
into the darkness –
Tonight do not make me
walk that road again

(*Ōtomo no Yakamochi*)

※

Dawn in the Imperial city –
I hear the *swish* of oars
and remember those fishing girls
from long ago

(*Anonymous*)

Alam Al-Mithral

I confess I was among the Elders
peering between the leaves at Susanna's nakedness
watching the light shine on her hair
as she washed it clean. I was there,
standing in the dust, under the cruel sun of Jeremiah.
I had come to steal the ripe figs
from Joakim's garden, for I was hungry
and my family poor. In my mind
I could taste the fruit of her. This is not
about lust. Of the Elders, I have nothing to say.
I left them at the crack in the wall
down on their knees. I have been to Aqaba
and Aleppo. I've seen the mark of Cain
on the brows of men, have heard the prophets
warn of the wrath of the Lord. I will wait
and see. Job says our days are swifter
than a weaver's shuttle and come to their end
without hope. For me, the miracle is of this body,
and in me until I lay it down I will carry
my sweet cargo, that sliver of paradise
glimpsed, once only, when I was a boy of fourteen.

Of Sappho / [shards] / *Sabi*

neither the sweetness of honey
nor the sting of bees

———

                         black sleep of night

———

like a fierce wind in the oak
love shakes my heart

———

                         evening star, most beautiful of all stars

———

dawn woke me

———

                         in the bright flame of noon
                         a cricket sings

———

                         when we meet
death lurks close by

———

                         take off your nightdress

———

between us the sea glistens
and shatters with waves

———

the hours   empty   endless

———

                    please   that moment
once again

———

                    gold greater than gold

———

the moon goes down
the Pleiades

———

                    alone
                    in a deepening night

Homage to the Presence
of the Mystery Among Us

All afternoon on the hillside above the hot springs,
dozing and reading, in the July heat, looking now
and then across the ravine to the large boulders
and mottled shade, not paying much attention,
just drowsing, drifting, daydreaming, letting
the scene wash over me without focusing,
without noticing until later that night,
staring into the fire, into the Roman
world of flames and ember, when
it came to me, that shape on the
ravine-side, in the shadows,
where I had been so long
in gazing – and where
finally now I see the
great antlered head
turn and the buck
rise to its feet
& disappear
into the
deeper
shade
of
day

Bible

The spider crab exults: *Look at me! I, too, am of the glory
of this world.* A field mouse turns to the snake: *This
is my body. This is my blood.* The scorpion scuttling
from under a rock, arms wide, pincers open, wants
to embrace us – it has news, friends – the tip
of its tail bears a psalm from Isaiah. And the heron
is Lord of the Apocalypse stalking across the pool,
choosing and stabbing: *This one. That one.
My chosen ones.*

Postcards to Cold Mountain

✥ MARKETPLACE, KUALA LUMPUR

The boy with a cleaver
with one sharp stroke
chops the live crab into two
dead halves
                    spilling out oily
glistening eggs, tiny suns
Its one large claw closing
and opening

✥ COCKPIT HOTEL, SINGAPORE

A voice "...*fuck me...yes...*" from the next room
A young Australian couple I had met at breakfast –
The way she ate her melon, shaving it
down with a spoon to where the tender, green skin
shone through

✥ NORTHERN TERRITORY, AUSTRALIA

In a Land Rover
50 miles southwest of Arnhem Land
immense marshlands, billabongs, ten thousand waterbirds
the great gene pool
genesis wonder
of wonders

Homage to Night

I will give you
anything – light
against white
stone, stark wheat
fields of Kárpathos
in the pit of summer –
I will give you
everything – sapphire
of the Unicorn
tapestry, lapis and
carnelian – I will give
you rain over
the moors, violet
of owl's clover,
the green of green
fields – I will
give you taste,
cinnamon, music
and touch, O night
outside, night
within – radiant night,
night inside the rose
of day, keening
night, teeming river
of absence, obsidian
sea, night each night
growing larger, opening –
everything, all things
I am and have
I will give to you
O night coming, night
ahead – exacting,
severe, honest
night.

Question and Answers

Why did you do it?

Because of those topaz mornings

Because of the weeping inside the marriage

Because of the fire and the rain and the fire

Because of the night train from Singapore to Kuala Lumpur

Because the peach, the spoon, the bowl, the cream, the sugar

Because my teachers were *pain* and *desire* and *almost*

Because of lions and gold and pearls in the wheat

Because the dog in my dream was the dog in my yard

Because my father turned in the doorway and looked back at me

Because of empire, silk sheets, cheap perfume, coins

Because of the great night over me each night

Because the monk sat there, serene, back straight, as his body
    went up in flames

Because the mynah bird kept repeating *You want me to* HURT *you?*

Because Ellen's chicken walked into my kitchen looking me over
    with its only eye

Because the panther tattooed on the bicep will rise in that other
    kingdom someday

Homage to the *Word-Hoard*

Lord help me but my mind's a blank today, only a few words
bubbling up, words like "no," or "glum," or "dull," but there must
be thousands of others down there, rattling their cages, clamoring
to get out, all kinds of words, big ones, scrawny ones, heroic and
muscular ones, coy, loony words, words tasting of cloves and
licorice, cross-dressed words wearing feathery boas, quantum
words, kaons and koans, singularities, black hole words sucking up
light, love, and loss, exploding words, supernovas, words like
wormholes into other worlds, ancient words, Neanderthal words
rubbing together to make fire, Cro-Magnon words rubbing
together to make magic, spells, incantations to sail the dead off to
the underworld, words that make the blind see, that make the lame
walk, words queuing in iambs, *vers libre* words playing tennis
without a net, and yes, I must admit it, bad words, embarrassing
words, words I dare not mention, and ugly words, too, words with
blackheads, wens, squatty warts sprouting tufts of stiff hairs,
blubbery words, Jean Paul Sartre words dripping *ennui*, words
smoking a cigarette, raising a Marlene Dietrich eyebrow and looking
down from a great height, words you wouldn't be caught dead
wearing, virgin words, cocky words, sluttish words, whispered-
in-the-car words, Etruscan words, words from lost tongues, words
with fur and teeth, wolf words wandering the plain bringing down
antelope, words that singe, sing, and burn, words that calm and
soothe, grunt words, snarls, guttural words, vocables and syllables,
words like the sound of doves murmuring in immemorial elms,
words crackling like fire, big sky words, cloud words, the clumsy
words of first love, words like lucre, like treasure, wedding words,
the keening words at gravesides, healing words, words tumbling
down in a waterfall of long golden hair, words you could climb,
words turning a toad to a prince, Stonehenge words, words lost in
the pit at Chichén Itzá, sweet Words run softly till I end my song,
these words I have shored against my ruins, words I would kneel
down before, all the way down, touching my forehead to the floor,

words like a guillotine, unswerving, absolute, words to keep from
going under, from breathing the dark waters, waiting words, maybe
a ship will pass by, an island will rise up, maybe this will be the day
I crawl ashore and you will see my wordprints in the sand leading
toward the jungle – *there* – the fronds rustling, closing behind where
I have disappeared into a new world, a luminous existence,
a world so perfect there's no purpose for a poem, no need for words.

Listening to Issa

This world of dew
and still
we fall in love

The crow walks
as if *he*
were tilling the field

I know I'm old –
but the flowering cherry trees
don't dislike me

Come on frog –
let's see you dance
to your own music

The oriole
wipes muddy feet
on the plum blossoms

Where are you
going in this *rain*
little snail?

Pissing –
I look down and see
a wild iris

The child
pulling a turnip with all his strength
topples backward

A crane
alights
on the garbage dump

In my hut
fireflies and mice
are friends

The old man
hobbles out
to look at flowers

So, moth –
this life –
are you happy with it?

How strange
to be alive
under the cherry blossoms

Am *I* next?
Is it *this* body you're cawing about
O crow?

This long night –
so very long –
praise Buddha

In every pearl
of dew
I see my home

Homage: Doo-Wop

There's so little sweetness in the music I hear now,
no croons, no doo-wop or slow ones where you could
hug up with someone and hold them against your body,
feel their heart against yours, touch their cheek
with your cheek – and it was OK, it was allowed,
even the mothers standing around at the birthday party,
the rug rolled back in the living room, didn't mind
if you held their daughters as you swayed to the music,
eyes squeezed shut, holding each other, and holding on
to the song, until you almost stopped moving,
just shuffled there, embracing, as the Moonglows
and Penguins crooned, and the mothers looked on
not with disapproval or scorn, looked on with their eyes
dreaming, as if looking from a thousand miles away, as if
from over the mountain and across the sea, a look
on their faces I didn't understand, not knowing then
those other songs I would someday enter, not knowing
how I would shimmer and writhe, jig like a puppet
doing the *shimmy-shimmy-kokobop*, or glide from turn
to counterturn within the waltz, not knowing
how I would hold the other through the night
and across the years, holding on for love and dear life,
for solace and kindness, learning the dance as we go,
learning from those first, awkward, shuffling steps,
that sweetness and doo-wop back at the beginning.

Directions

How weary, stale, flat, and unprofitable
Seem to me all the uses of this world

Take a plane to London.
From King's Cross take the direct train to York.
Rent a car and drive across the vale to Ripon,
then into the dales toward the valley of the Nidd,
a narrow road with high stone walls on each side,
and soon you'll be on the moors. There's a pub,
The Drovers, where it's warm inside, a tiny room,
you can stand at the counter and drink a pint of Old Peculiar.
For a moment everything will be all right. You're back
at a beginning. Soon you'll walk into Yorkshire country,
into dells, farms, into blackberry and cloud country.
You'll walk for hours. You'll walk the freshness
back into your life. This is true. You can do this.
Even now, sitting at your desk, worrying, troubled,
you can gaze across Middlesmoor to Ramsgill,
the copses, the abbeys of slanting light, the fells,
you can look down on that figure walking toward Scar House,
cheeks flushed, curlews rising in front of him, walking,
making his way, working his life, step by step, into grace.

Oh Yes

Oh no –
now we're in for it, everything's slamming shut,
closing shop, the leaves on the cottonwood are crying
fuck it and letting go in the wind, the cold
is coming, winter storms are massing at sea,
morning ice on the deck and the dog skids off
in a blur of legs, then it rains and rains and rains,
and the plague is upon us, strange fevers and aches,
the body spelling it out, impossible to ignore,
you're in a machine consuming itself,
and this morning walking out, you look up
at the persimmon tree for the first time in weeks
and notice all the leaves are gone, and there they are –
persimmons – fiery globes, hosannas and lauds,
and you can't help yourself, admit it, even sick
and miserable, mired in the dreck of winter,
you reach out your hand, take hold of the fruit,
oh yes, there's another world, there's a sun
within the sun, yes, kindness is real,
oh yes, blessings are everywhere.

Homage: Summer/Winter, Shay Creek

IN THE SHINING

I've got my chair and a good book and I'm sitting
out behind the cabin in a shaft of sunlight, reading.
A couple of Steller's jays who might be my friends
perch themselves on branches in the ponderosa
and sugar pine. They can't read the book I've got
but they can read me, and they watch very carefully
for that moment when my hand reaches in
to my pocket and pulls out some crusts of bread
which I toss out over the forest floor and the jays
spring off the limbs and streak down in a blue blaze,
scoop the crusts and are back in the limbs again
chortling. This is the way of my life these days –
lazing, serene, but not so indolent, not so torpid
that I won't get up now and then, grab my chair,
and move to another spot, over there by the cedar,
to that new place shining now in the sun.

Everywhere, *everywhere*, snow sifting down,
a world becoming white, no more sounds,
no longer possible to find the heart of the day,
the sun is gone, the sky is nowhere, and of all
I wanted in life – so be it – whatever it is
that brought me here, chance, fortune, whatever
blessing each flake of snow is the hint of, I am
grateful, I bear witness, I hold out my arms,
palms up, I know it is impossible to hold
for long what we love of the world, but look
at me, is it foolish, shameful, arrogant to say this,
see how the snow drifts down, look how happy
I am.

Alchemy: Final Music

Death was some thing the old poems
sang about. *Timor mortis...*
Ubi sunt qui ante nos fuerunt?...
Carpe diem... Donne's portrait
in his shroud he hung above his head
those last days. Full fathom five
thy father lies. Coral and eyes.
Worldes bliss ne last no throwe.
It wit and wend away anon.
Poets measuring with words
the wordless process the body
proceeds with. With night.
With mourning. Love labors against it,
losing. The mind over the years
gradually accedes, succeeds, perhaps,
in having a past to build from,
to place against. A negative. The image
appearing gradually from chemicals
in the dark in the red light.
Like those songs. All the old poems
growing clearer as we grow older.

Steps to the River

(versions from the ancient Sanskrit & Tamil)

Friend
this night makes music of me
of my body
just as the wind makes flute songs
through the shining holes of bamboo
bored by those black bees
from the land where he dwells

❦

Her young body is like an island
Her beauty the waves that continually break upon it
There is a hidden place
a hut of tendrils and vines
in whose moist shade even now
the drowsy god of love
begins to stir

❦

Everyone in the village asleep
except us
all night hearing
the blue-sapphire flowers
tearing loose from branches
falling all night
as the two of us
listen

❦

Impossible to measure
my love for that man from the mountains
where the black stalk of the *kuṟiñci*
flowers every twelve years
and of its pollen bees make their richest honey

⚜

The jingling from her anklets stops
Her lover, tired, rolls onto his back
And now the room chimes
with the sound of tiny bells
from the belt around her waist

⚜

Over here the sheets smell of musk
over there a stain of henna
disheveled here, kohl marks there
crushed flowers in the blankets
everywhere clues of her postures
from the night before

⚜

Lover of pollen, you are trapped
The struggling bee makes the petals
close around him

⚜

They didn't speak
No art was involved
Just the touch of his hand
the loosening of her skirt

In a moment
it was over

☙

She lifted her arms to undo her hair
and glanced at me with shining eyes
I swear, friend, even the blossoms of water lilies
catch fire

☙

Dear, don't feel so smug
because he's painted your portrait
He might have done mine as well
but the brush kept trembling in his hand

☙

The one from his height looks down
believing he is great
The other from the ground looks up
believing he is poor

☙

Little cuckoo
don't sing until you can fly
The crows around here are vicious
toward any song
other than their own

☙

You gave me feet the long road wears down
You gave me a wife who left me
You gave me this body time burns to ashes
You gave me a voice for begging
Lord, when will you weary of all your gifts?

❦

Like glittering waves on water
the boasters and loudmouths
get everyone's attention
If you seek the pearl
hold your breath
and dive deep

❦

A village wall in winter
where the children of the poor
freezing in tattered rags
shove and huddle together
in the one spot the sun warms

❦

The frog clears its throat
squinches forward
and leaps
mouth open wide
toward a swarm of flies
hovering above the dungpile

❦

No money
No wisdom
No merit
The story of my life
and now the jig is up

※9

Like a heavy temple bell
struck hard
death claims a good man
And his love resonates after
shimmering through our lives

3
Crossing Over

Memories at the Movies

Malle's *Phantom India* makes you look at the vulture
feeding on the buffalo carcass, its featherless
fleshy neck smeared with blood, the entire screen
an image of curved hooking beak, ripping
and gulping bits of entrails. You look away,
cover your eyes, hoping the scene will change.
When you glance again, there's the bloated corpse
and flies and greedy inflamed eye of the buzzard
which now plunges its whole head and neck
into the buffalo's asshole, picking out coils of intestine.
The camera doesn't move, the film continues to scroll.
Eventually you have to look, you've *paid*
to see this mess, but the more you look the less
distant it is – the deeper into it, the more it becomes
un-ugly, becomes just bird feeding on body,
until you're cleaned out, gutted, empty inside yourself,
fighting back all those memories of her,
of being in this same theater, shoulder
to shoulder in the dark, deep into *Les Enfants
du Paradis, Jules et Jim* – all unreeled at last now,
the film coiling on the projection floor as you sit
in the present with your head plunged
into memories, the way love will leave you,
unspooled, the way you become your own vulture
tearing and feasting on the past.

Notes Toward a 19th-Century Painting

Begin with light –
the water a silvery grey against the far shore,
a glassy green in the major body edged with ebony,
late afternoon mist blurring the shape of distant fir,
the sleek back of a whale barely visible in the channel.
In the lower foreground an island emerges,
then a cabin tilting above shoreline on a croppage of rocks.
Three figures stand around a cairn –
two men and a woman, their postures discrete, private.
One, his back to us, drunk, stares out toward the whale.
The woman, slightly apart, with sharp almost Indian features,
gazes furiously at some place far and cold within her.
The last figure, eyes attentive to his hands, sharpens an axe.
The clouded sky swirls, textured like marble.
On the horizon, volcanic peaks. Beyond them, emptiness.
How small the figures appear in the painting.
How persistently the perspective sweeps our eyes back to them,
hesitating, suggesting something about to happen,
as if someone were going to step out of the silence,
as if there were something to say.

Cézanne and the Noumenal World

Dusk, gold and blues – the haystacks of Monet – his water lilies
shimmering in the texture of light. Like Debussy. Who wouldn't
eat from that plate. Or Gauguin – his islands and women
and the red flowers and blue horses and the green sea.
Van Gogh's night astonished with stars, the black of blackbirds
in yellow wheat, a sky in torches of black flame.
Seurat dabbing the tip of a brush ten thousand times
to give us the molecular blaze of figures on the Grand Jatte.
Renoir's nudes — flesh an opal fire glazed with pearl.

But it's Cézanne
who troubles me – his architecture of color, sculpture of light –
Cézanne who tried to carve the flow of the world in canvas.
His still lifes – so careful, so slow   the grapes and pears turned
before he could finish. So he turned to the mountain, every day
for years confronting Sainte-Victoire, attempting the substance
of granite, a structure outside seasons.

In his studio at the end,
an old man, dying, he hobbled over canvases strewn on the floor,
Sainte-Victoire wavering now – trees and cliffs washing out,
the great mountain inside him fading – spoiling like the fruit
on the table – alchemized in the core of the flesh.

Portrait of the Artist as a Young Boy

The boy is making something
for the girl he has a crush on
he has taken an old panel of wood

and with a pencil draws an island
with trees a horse rearing up
flashing its hooves toward the sun

all of it surrounded by a sea
which he shapes in scallops and curves
then he takes a magnifying glass

and traces the pencil lines with
sunlight focused to a laser point
burning into the wood the outline

of horse and trees island and sea
he stops now and then to close
his eyes which burn as if

the drawing is being etched
through them seared
into his skull into his mind

which persists in its vision
forcing the boy back to his task
forcing the sun to char

the wood to brand the shapes
of the boy's world into the grain
that wants to catch fire

blaze up and burn into ash
what the boy would make of love
what love makes of him

Waiting for the Barbarians

The old man in the café could have been Cavafy –
the way the cup trembled in his hand, the ardor
in his eyes behind thick glasses, his furtive glances
toward the young man. The old poet looked
so out of place sitting among ferns and oak furniture,
Coltrane's *A Love Supreme* smoldering from speakers.
The young man sat across from me, long ponytail,
a diamond in his earlobe, dour mouth.
                                    I moved
my queen across the board, through a landscape littered
with knights and pawns. I thought of the ancient city
of Alexandria, a room above the Arab quarter, a man
imagining his life as a series of candles – a few up ahead
lit and shining, an army strung out behind, burnt down,
wisps of smoke curling like incense into the room.
The man sits there conjuring his youth when Eros
ruled all his blood.
                        Cavafy, I know you're just a shade
in the underworld of language. All day I've been sitting here,
waiting for moves, for insight on how to proceed. The old man
still looks our way, but he is bored and tired. Coltrane's fire
has been returned to silence. Across from me
the young man keeps raising his head, his face sullen, eyes
without expression, as game after game we isolate, humiliate,
and murder our kings.

Shine

I climbed the ladder into the spring morning
and stood swaying among bees blazing in honeysuckle,
my pruning shears butchering vines so rank they bent
the trellis. Stretching, I balanced on the ladder, reaching out
over the edge, into the flames of honeysuckle, cottonwood
shimmering a green fire, leaning into a slow motion
of shears thudding to the deck, the ladder away from me
going over – and the bottom dropped out – body
flailing, I watched myself fall, watched as my arm stiffened
to brace body weight, palm smacking the wood deck,
a shock of force jolting my arm out of its socket –
I writhed on the deck, guttering and retching, my arm
a grotesque angle from its shoulder – then
the slow drive to the hospital, all things in rapture,
a paraclete of tongues, the nurse's face suffused with light,
pain grinding me back into my life, past sorrow, back
into the blood hum of my body, into the dragon shine.

Shape-Shifter

She strolls to the supermarket – to the Shopping Bag, Pico Rivera, going to check out the butcher stall, the windows of meat, T-bones and pork chops, *chorizo*, chicken claws – wearing short-shorts and red open-toed pumps, painted toenails, lipstick smeared over the lip lines, crucifix dangling from a thin gold chain around her neck. The shoppers think it's Babette, their neighbor's teenage daughter, they don't see the tongue, the oil glaze of the eyes. A group of boys slouch around the magazine rack, hair thick with pomade and slicked into ducktails. She saunters past. Smirking, one of the boys drops a nickel at her feet. She stoops to pick it up, loose blouse drooping open. The boys squint and peer down, until she rises, face flushed, smiling, and drops the coin into the boy's open palm, where it glints and burns like a bit of chipped-off scale.

◆§ 1987

The boy is thirteen or so, dressed in a black T-shirt, black Levi's. From his left earlobe a silver spider dangles on a thin chain. He's standing at the San Lorenzo rivermouth, his arm around his girlfriend. She has braces, fishnet stockings, burgundy tank top, the beginning of breasts. They are both smiling, both crazy with love. My dog runs around them, crazed with the smell of their happiness. Seagulls scream and scatter from the energy of the dog. Waves smash onto shore, set after set, the long reach of winter storms from Alaska. There's a hard undertow, sludging sand and crushed shells back into the bay. The water ploughs around my feet and I sink quickly to my ankles. It's as if I'm moving, as if something is tugging me from under, tearing me away from this young couple. The loud surf drowns the cries of the gulls, waves curl in a long serpentine motion down the beach, a fire of glittering scales on the water in the bright sun.

Sky Diving

A morning in autumn, years ago. I was living out back in the shed,
the pony barn we called it, a simple whitewashed room full of
windows, with a bed, woodstove, bookshelves, a desk. I was in bed
looking up through the skylight, past the bare branches of the
walnut trees, into the sky where a group of seagulls rode a thermal
in a huge rotating gyre. I was thinking about the skydiver with a
camera strapped to his back, a filmmaker, who the week before
leaped after a group of divers who had formed a great circle in the
sky – which he plunged into, spinning the camera around. The TV
news had shown the footage. I was thinking of this when Sarah
called out my name and walked into the shed. I can still see her,
standing there, blue jeans and sandals, white T-shirt, her hair damp
from a shower, smelling of balsam and resin. She had recently
returned from Germany, leaving her husband, beginning the
divorce, the ugly struggle. She stood there, hesitant, embarrassed,
saying the words she must have rehearsed. I could not cross over.
I couldn't even manage the dignity of a *no*. I just let the moment
move into the larger day, into the season and the years that have
brought me here. I let her stand there to make small talk, to listen
as I told her about the news program, how the divers broke off from
their circle, doing backflips, tumbles, a crude aerial ballet. And then
the part in the film where their chutes unravel and they are suddenly
jerked up out of sight while the camera continues to record – the
wobbling horizon, ground enlarging from below, the landscape
beginning to swing crazily – and you realize something's wrong, the
cameraman is out of control. On the morning of the jump, among
the crowd and confusion, he hadn't been paying attention,
distracted, thinking maybe of his cameras and lenses, and didn't put
on his chute, which he realized only when he reached for the cord.
And there I was talking away, wondering aloud what his thoughts
were those last moments plunging into the uprushing ground –
while Sarah stood there, the expression on her face looking at me –
our own time and terror crashing down with us as we hurtled to
earth.

In the Dragon's Mouth

I'm sitting under a palapa at the Beach of the Dead watching the
different blues of the sea and the sunlight shattering on waves –
when this man walks up to me, a stranger, looks kind of like a
beach bum, cutoff jeans, dirty T-shirt, worn pair of flip-flops,
comes up and greets me like an old friend, sits down in the other
chair and begins to tell me how the tourist women aren't worth the
effort – there was this one Australian whom he let stay with him,
for free, in his small jungle house down at La Boca, took her out
snorkeling in his outboard, bought her dinners, drinks, introduced
her to the Vallarta scene, spent long hours talking with her, *real
talks*, about the past, hopes, last night's nightmare, and after a week
of this, after dinner at his place and a bottle of good wine, which is
impossible to find in this part of Mexico, he stands up and asks her
if he can hug her, and she says "OK but you're not going to screw
me," *screw me, she actually said that, and of course I wanted to, had
wanted to the whole bloody week, so we hugged and I went to bed, pissed
off, and she left the next morning,* and he stops talking to swat at
some sand flies on his legs and I notice that my legs have tiny pin
pricks of blood on them, he tells me it's the no-see-ums, *take a lime
and rub the juice over your skin,* and I look at the man again, chipped
front tooth, hair uncombed, beer belly, friendly face, and he tells
me he was born in North Dakota, went back five years ago, bought
a small farm, planted some dope, got busted, jumped bail, *and now
I do carpentry work around Seattle, winters I come down here, the
weather's great, it's easy to find a cheap place, I live good for four or five
months, then head back to the Northwest,* and so we sit here, watching
the sea, as the day grows toward sunset, the sun spreads out over
the maw of the bay, finally he stops talking, the night comes down
around us, and we stop seeing, we can only hear the sound of
waves and the thin whine of mosquitoes, I feel my heart pumping
salty blood all through me, I sit here, taking it in, giving back
nothing, letting the night have its way, the air humid with a fetid

jungle odor, like the breath of an animal, just sit here, afraid I am losing something, no future, no past, just the two of us, sitting alone in the present, slaughtering time.

Venom

It had to happen, it *has* to happen.
This time it was Steve.
The doctor said *melanoma*
and all the doors into the bright mornings
began slamming shut.
I remember how embarrassed he was, *I* was,
when we met on the path coming up from the cabin.
A summer day, the garden going crazy with squash and beans,
the corn stalks a green Gauguin never found in paradise.
I remember our eyes met quickly,
quickly looked away,
to the garden, to the ground, to the seeping faucet,
the slick shine of water disappearing,
soaking into the earth.
Well, he said.
And months later in an Indian ashram
seeking a miracle,
Steve,
someone told me this,
pointed to the photo of the guru on the wall,
– accusation? recognition? –
pointed his finger at it,
as if there were something profound in the gesture,
something outside language,
beyond meaning,
and his life just
left him.

It was the way the skunk looked at me
after my dog mauled it
the night it tried to raid the chicken hutch.
I was in the kitchen, reading,
when the night tore itself apart.
I rushed outside –
the dog whimpered around the yard,
scrubbing her face on the ground.
Then I saw the skunk, struggling to move,
dragging its hind legs.
When I approached, it stopped,
looked up at me.
The whole yard smelled of burnt rubber.
Holy Christ, I muttered.
It continued to look at me,
no pleading, no anger,
no fear on its face.
One dying creature
looking at another.
I knew I had to do something –
half its guts trailed from its belly.
I got the shovel, the new one,
and held the tip above the skunk's neck.
It continued to stare.
I thrust down, trying to sever the head.
It took three blows.
The dog rubbed against my leg.
Sad, angry, disgusted,
I gave a swift kick,
missed,
and stood leaning against the shovel
wondering what do I do now,
what's next,
what do I do with this mess,

this body.
The dog yowled, whined,
unable to rid the smell from her muzzle.
I called to her,
held out my hand, touched her head,
calmed her.
Then walked to the corner of the yard
where the limbs of the pear tree,
heavy with fruit,
bent down almost to the ground.
I stuck the blade of the shovel into the earth
and began to dig.

How Green the Leaves in Sunlight Arc

On the phone with my friend who is having
a hard time with his life, who sits in a chair for days
holding a knife in his lap, who isn't able to talk
about it. It might be *bipolar*, but there is no word
for where he is. He is calling from the crack
between worlds, where the barrio of East L.A.
smacks up against New Asia, where the voices
he hears all day speak in tongues, and his life,
his other life, is lived in another country, and what
do you know of it, he asks, what language do you speak?
And I am listening hard, trying to piece it together,
trying to find the mystery of it, listening as I stare
into the green leaves of the plant outside the window,
and I notice for the first time that it's dying –
I look closer and see insects, tiny *grotesques*, colonies
of them, who've drilled their mouths into the veins
of the plant, whose bodies are the color of the leaves –
and it's hopeless, I'm thinking, everywhere it's
the everyday wreckage, the coming apart from within,
wormseed, Death smirking in the glaze of sunlight,
stroking the blade, Death who would have us
slit our throats with diamonds, whispering – *Do it,
do it, there's nothing here worth holding to,
you've already heard the story, all of it, you know
how it ends* – and what shall I tell my friend
whose voice drills into my skull, what new story,
what poem shall I construct, what should I tell him
about love, about how to pass through, tell me,
what shall I say about the crossing over, *bipolar*,
about what's on the other side of the crack,
about that island of ice and snow where the shades
hold out their cups, thirsty for what we bring,
our elixir, our mixture of honey and milk and blood,
our memories of how green the leaves are in the sun.

Death in the Tehachapi

Mr. Cox would fall asleep in the armchair still gripping
his drink. He'd doze awhile, come to, take a sip, then
drift off again. Someone stoked wood in the fireplace.
Hunters came in with shotguns and dead quail. Then
a smell of coffee and potatoes frying in a black skillet.
Mr. Cox waking and nodding, weaving in and out of it,
clutching his drink, the one he invented, a glass of gin
and crushed ice topped with burgundy, the wine
drifting down like a thick cloud the color of blood.
Outside, a vicious Tehachapi wind. A poker game inside,
money on the table, half a dozen men playing for keeps,
now and then someone gazing toward the armchair,
the anchor of that room, the polestar, hunters and hunted,
Death stalking slowly, spectral, coming in for the kill.

Knots

Trying to tie my shoes, clumsy, not able to work out
the logic of it, fumbling, as my father stands there
his anger growing over a son who can't even do
this simplest thing for the first time, can't even manage
the knot to keep his shoes on – *You think someone's*
going to tie your shoes for you the rest of your life? –
No, I answer, forty-five years later, tying my shoe,
hands trembling with this memory. My father
and all those years of childhood not being able to work out
how he loved me, a knot so tight it has taken all my life
to untie.

Grief

Went to the Wailing Wall of the Jerusalem within me.
My father was there, weeping. My mother was there, wailing
and weeping. The little boy I was, sobbing and pleading.
The prophet was there, predicting ruin, the falling of mountains.
The walls of the city, the portals of the body, collapsing.
Went weeping to the Wall of the death of my brother's daughter.
Stood in the courtyard among the moneychangers
listening to the sound of coins changing hands,
the city everywhere around me in flames, the graves
open, Apocalypse coming down, and rain like a black fire.

Craft

The boy playing in the plaza is now being beaten
by his father. A terrible whipping and the boy is screaming,
sobbing. The other Gypsies look on with indifference,
except for a burro who has turned, still chewing, and gazes
with its large eyes from some other world. Who knows
what the child has done. The father drags him off
still howling, but without fervor now, the worst of it
over. The silence of the noon gradually returns
as the heart calms. The mind continues its labor
chiseling away at the Andalucían light, carving out a day
in a mountain of days, working at it, considering
whether to shape the cries and the burro. Or not.

Feral

The plaza of the Gypsies. Under the ruined castle. A spring
pouring into a stone basin where burros and horses drink.
Since before the time of Cervantes. A taverna. Fierce
sunlight at noon. The plaza empty. Absolute stillness.
Even the cicadas stunned by the heat. A plate of olives,
goat cheese, cucumber. Cobblestones and whitewashed
walls. A day like marble. Solstice. Crushed rosemary.
Holding on with everything I have. Wheat fields
the color of fawn. Bread. Black figs. Gripping
hard, with mind and heart clenching, holding on to
what's human. This moment. This place where I make
my strict joy.

Crossing the Island

(Kárpathos, twenty years ago)

Heat heat and the sky a flame of sapphire
an ocean of fire even rocks blazing
the earth a rush of coals Aegean summer
the air still the day dead center in the sun
the world without breath even the goats
drinking light all morning have descended
to the shade of a cistern while out there
the blue of the ocean and the other blue of sky
come together in that place where the gods
descend to this world and enter
the heavy honey of the body and it was on
this day when I set out into the core of light
wondering what it would bring for I knew
for once and for good my marriage was over
and henceforth there would be only these excursions
into the sun into the body and the world
would exact its praise of basil or goats or the smell
of thyme and the resin and gold pitch of pine
and all the shelters of the spirit began crumbling
within me as I dismantled the man I was
learning to replace the old belief of Latin
with the new tongue of this world the tongue
of rock and mountain and memory of the woman
washing her hair on the terrace in the granite light
as I went through the day to the other
end of the island where the wedding guests
had butchered a goat and roasted the meat
over a fire in a noon so bright I couldn't see
the flames as if sunlight were searing the flesh
and the bride looked upon it all and found it

to her liking as the groom carved the meat
passed it around and we ate of the world
and so it would continue

Seizure

Dawn in the San Joaquin, I get out of the car
to stretch and let the dog romp awhile in a field
when my body suddenly begins to stutter, quake
uncontrollably, and part of me watches, detached,
thinking   *is this a heart attack? a stroke?* –
as my trunk and limbs buck and flail and I
keel onto my back, convulsing. After a time
I see the dog across the field chasing something
and who I am comes back to my body
which has quieted, and I lie on the ground,
cheek against the earth, my ear listening to a pulse
from the underworld that gradually becomes
my heart. I pull myself up, hold on to the car door
as the dog trots over, tongue out, happy, and me too,
happy to be in this field below the Gold Country,
a moment in spring, in the 53rd year of my life,
wondering what it was that broke open the morning,
scattering incandescence everywhere, the trees
across the way still pulsing, shimmering as if in flames,
and within my body a hushed feeling, beatitude,
a silence closing around silence.

Lines

I wasn't about to believe her – this seer, this psychic –

and wondered what she would say as she read the lines
in my palm. I didn't want to know about my future –
I was still puzzling over the past – the future seemed
obvious, a fierce ravenous engine railing around the bend.
The seer, drunk under the winter night, squinted

over my open palm, and I admit it shook a little,
a slight tremble, nothing much. I could feel
my heart pump the blood down through my arm.
I tried to resist this miracle, tried not to be obvious
about my own gaze at the arm of the psychic –

the needle marks, the tracks in the veins in the soft
crease of skin above her forearm. I was thinking
maybe she should try her skill at reading those lines –
how far into the future *they* led. She worked
at a Crisis Center, eight years answering a phone

and counseling the lonely, the drunks, the suicidal
who wanted a witness, who didn't want to die alone –
The memory and horror of one call, silence on the line,
then the *crack* of a pistol.
Her gift was well-known – police consulted her

for clues to murders – perhaps she could envision
where the body of the little boy might be,
In the bushes down the ravine outside Boulder Creek.
But she never got it quite right – she was accurate
about the fire road and the gnarled manzanita –

but the body was in the next county. So I wasn't
greatly worried as she began to trace my lines –
How this one meant I had lived a rich life, and where
this one forked meant someone close to me had died
and a part of me had died also, and this jagged line, this scar

cutting across the others – *This one is the love line –*
You've been lucky, you've had a great love in your life –
See here, how the line leaves the palm, traces
the air, how it zigs and zags, rising, seeking,
rises toward the sharp points of stars,

crosses the zodiac, connecting planets and nebulae
into the shapes of beasts drifting across night – an amazing love –
And she's weeping now, holding my palm, squeezing it,
hard, clutching and talking about love, how she can't see
where it's going, where it ends, and I'm sitting there,

dumbly, looking at her, wondering about this, not so much
interested in where it's going, or where it's been, but where
is it – what's it doing in my life, in hers – and suddenly
I begin to believe she might be right – how it's here,
now, right *here*, in the clasping, sweating, scarred

palms of our hands, bridged together, holding on.

Auvergne

Oc, Dieu d'amor
Quora me donas jòi, quora m'en ven dolor

– RAMBAUD DE VAQUEIRÀS

Why should the mindless singing
of the mockingbird high in the avocado tree
so much please me? Or the lure of light
these winter mornings the first days of War? –
as our Century comes down.
                        I sit on a bench
reading the eight-hundred-year-old poems of a Sufi dervish.
So where is the Beloved Friend? Is it this dog
sleeping at my feet under the shadow of a cow skull
nailed to the fence?
                        I believe
I no longer believe in the romance of the body.
Once, twenty years ago, in that other country,
in Auvergne, I knelt down inside the fire.
Of my beloved, I remember most her quiet words,
the taste of comice, warm rain in the orchard,
our little happiness inside us. That's not the All
of it. Rumi says, *The price of a kiss from the Beloved*
is your life. What a bargain! But I was a thief,
I did not pay.
                        Like everybody,
like you, I returned from that country of love
alive. From nights of the Auvergne. The river Lot
with its shade trees in summer, arbors of dusty grapes,
white honey from the blossoms of rosemary,
fields where the dragon sang inside the writhing
mouths of poppies where the black seeds catch fire.

                    Returned
to the mockingbird, crazed, singing out of season.
To my dog, stretching now, who turns
and shoves her snout over my book, jowls
slobbering on Rumi's ecstatic poem to the Beloved.
                    What
does she know, this trusting, dumb creature
who forgives me everything? Is *The cure for pain*
in the pain? Grinning, tongue out, tail thrashing,
she knows something is up.
                    In the next Millennium,
among the nightmares and machines, among time's
indifferent slaughter of our body, there must be poems
to make room of silence, to praise birdsong in winter light,
to sing of Auvergne, the Friend, and the old promises of love.

Crossing Over and Back

How *triste* the façades of the *palacios* along the Grand Canal.
And those crowds back and forth crossing the Bridge of Sighs.
Where is the other shore? This boat goes to San Michele,
the isle of the dead. No one gets off but me and two old
Russian women. They bear flowers for Stravinsky's tomb.
We walk together among the graves searching for the dead.
Good luck, I say. They smile – *Spaseba.* The one
I'm looking for is difficult to find, as he would have wished.
*Most poems fail not through craft but from a failure
of character.* He said that. At last I find a simple stone
imbedded in the earth – the chiseled name *Ezra Pound.*
No epitaph. No famous quote. Someone has planted
a laurel nearby, but it withers in this Venetian swelter.
I say the goodbye I have carried for many years.
What is it that I still cherish? I think to myself walking back
with those two old peasant women, kindness etched
in their faces, wondering how we have been compressed
to the elementals of language, to gestures of respect
and goodwill, to the poem's chiseled music.

By the Rivers of Babylon

for my brothers, Mike & Tim

I walk the levee of the San Lorenzo,
a midsummer afternoon,
walking to the clinic for the lab results.
I see the heron wrapped in its shroud of silence,
shoulders hunched, standing over a pool,
gazing into its still spirit.
This day my blood will be translated
into an alphabet spelling *no going back.*
This day with the ashes of my mother in the Pacific.
This day with the ashes of my father in the Sierra.
What are you waiting for? *What are you waiting for?*
Never before the arc of the hummingbird
like a streaking evanescent jewel.
Never before this world so translated from plural to singular.
Not the leaves of the cottonwood,
but each leaf,
dazzling with light.
I walk to the clinic
where the doctor waits with his map of the future:
the body, the body,
the elemental process of the body –
to be trolled for, to take the lure,
gladly,
baited with worm,
the line dangling from the great cloud ship of myth,
to be caught
and held squirming and gasping in the tight body,
then released, tossed back
into the glittering, streaming river
of this day.

I crossed the Mekong at dusk,
the outskirts of Vientiane –
in the street a car on its back,
an immense scarab, its carapace in flames,
black oily smoke smudging the sky,
and everywhere soldiers of the Pathet Lao.
In the morning
I woke with sunlight shattering through cracks in the walls,
splinters of light,
the room sheathed in cobwebs,
like a cocoon of silken fire.
In the marketplace
the Royalists and Pathet Lao laid down their weapons.
I looked into a bucket pulsing with toads,
another squirming with what appeared to be intestines –
eels with tiny eyes and needled teeth.
On a table the hacked pieces of a large lizard.
Everything of this earth as food,
what we put into our mouths,
the flesh of crabs,
mangos, cow tongue, words…

❦

We strolled the banks of the Ganges near the summer palace.
We could see smoke scurling downriver
from pyres on the Manikarnika ghat.
Günnar talked of his pilgrimage to Bodh Gayā,
of his studies in the secret tantras of eros.
He had meditated under the bo tree.
He had seen a body rise.
We all wanted miracles.
The Ganges, sluggish and muddy, offered nothing.

We wandered the chowk,
lost in its labyrinth of alleys,
loud processions bearing corpses to the river,
Sadhus smeared with ashes chanting *Rama nama satya hai* –
the name of God is truth,
or so Günnar translated it.
Just as we tried translating the scrawl of human smoke
unscrolling above the burning ghats –
Death opens the flower.
The body's marriage burns down.
The flowering bride wakes in the long corridor of ash.
And so

❦

I hold my father in the elemental form of ash
where the granite river of the Sierra plunges into the Mojave.
Black bear, cougar, coyote in these mountains for thousands of years
where my two brothers and I have come together.
Below the Paiute graveyard overlooking the river canyon
Tim scatters our father's ashes to the South,
the North,
to the bluff where the sun rises,
to the West.
A sudden wind
and the ashes gust back over us,
dusting our faces and clothes,
a faint smell and taste of my father in my own body,
in this blaze of flesh,
these three flames of men burning out of their lives,
fathering in each other the elemental love
of brother for brother.

❦

I walk the levee of the San Lorenzo
where the river empties into the sea.
Thinking of my father.
Thinking of my mother whose ashes years ago were strewn
over these waters.
She lives only in the minds of a few now,
and soon there will be no one alive
who knew her,
she will no longer walk in anyone's dream
as I walk now along this shore
while miles out and deep under water
on the edge of the Monterey trench
something monolithic moves in darkness,
silent,
plunging huge and fast.
And above it the killers,
orcas,
arc the surface,
a pod hunting together
down from Canada
tracing the song and spoor of whale.
I walk the levee under the long arc of the sun
with all my past streaming through me,
those mornings of light, the cottonwoods
with their ten thousand tongues murmuring of summer
and the slow burning of seasons.
I walk along the river,
towing it all
huge and singing
into the alchemy of this day.

NOTES

Provenance [pages 5–9]   *puñal*: Dagger.
Palacio Real: Royal Palace.
Madrileños: Citizens of Madrid.

Matar la Noche [page 22]   *matar la noche*: "To kill the night," a phrase
Madrileños use to describe the nightlife of Madrid,
which lasts until early morning.

Hacedor [page 23]   *hacedor*: The maker, the artist.

In the Maze Garden of the   *Generalife*: The summer palace of the sultans above
Generalife [page 26]   the Alhambra in Granada.

And for This Also I am   *Pondicherry*: A city in southern India on the Bay of
Ashamed [page 31]   Bengal.

From Time to Time Turning   *Tomatlán de la Boca*: A fishing village in Jalisco,
My Head to See [page 32]   Mexico.

Die Schwermut [page 33]   *Die Schwermut*: "Despair"; the title of a poem by
Trakl.

The Words of Chilam Balam   *Chilam Balam*: Priest/prophet Jaguar; Jaguar Priest.
[page 33]   Mayan prophet of Apocalypse who lived to witness
his prophecy with the coming of the Spaniards. The
Books of Chilam Balam are all that have survived of
the principal sacred texts of the Mayans.

Earth Angel [page 35]   *Earth Angel*: The title of a song by the Penguins, a
rhythm & blues group of the fifties.

Waking on the Shining Path   *Ayacucho*: A Peruvian city in the Andes within the ter-
[page 36]   ritory of the Marxist guerrilla group Shining Path.

Love Like a Catch of Fire   Lady Izumi Shikibu and Prince Atsumichi were part
[page 38]   of the Imperial Heian court at the turn of the tenth
century in Japan. Their great love was celebrated in
many poems to each other.

These Nights, Passing Through [page 38]	*Netania Davrath*: Soprano who recorded *Songs of the Auvergne* orchestrated by Joseph Canteloube (Vanguard Classics OVC 8001/2).
Our Blood is Red Coral... [page 41]	The sentence is from Kazantzakis. Kárpathos is a Greek island in the Dodecanese.
Autumn [page 52]	*Man'yōshū*: Earliest collection of Japanese poetry, containing 4,516 poems, compiled in the late eighth century.
Alam Al-Mithral [page 53]	*Alam Al-Mithral*: Arabic word with no equivalent in English; refers to the "place" where images exist.
Of Sappho/[shards]/Sabi [pages 54–55]	*Sabi* (Japanese): The patina, the character, the stark beauty that time gradually works into an object.
Steps to the River [pages 71–75]	These versions are derived and adapted from the translations of Professor H.H. Ingalls (*Sanskrit Poetry*, Harvard University Press) and Professor George L. Hart (*The Poems of Ancient Tamil*, University of California Press).
Death in the Tehachapi [page 94]	*Tehachapi*: Region where the Sierra Nevada descends to the Mojave.
Auvergne [pages 104–105]	*Auvergne*: Region in France that was once part of Occitania where twelfth-century Provençal troubadours composed the first lyric poetry in a modern European language. *Rambaud de Vaqueiràs*: An early troubadour.
Crossing Over and Back [page 106]	*Spaseba*: "Thank-you" (Russian).
By the Rivers of Babylon [pages 107–110]	*Vientiane*: Capital of Laos. *Pathet Lao*: Communist forces that overcame the Royalists in 1975.

Ghats **Steps**. Manikarnika ghat is the main location of the funeral pyres in Varanasi (Benares) where the corpses of Hindu devotees are cremated and whose ashes are then strewn into the Ganges.

Bodh Gayā: The place in Bengal where Siddhartha Gautama attained enlightenment under the bo tree.

ABOUT THE AUTHOR

Joseph Stroud was born in 1943. His previous books are *In the Sleep of Rivers* (Capra Press, 1974) and *Signatures* (BOA Editions, 1982). He lives part of the time in Santa Cruz on the California coast, part of the time in a cabin at Shay Creek on the east side of the Sierra Nevada.

BOOK DESIGN & composition by John D. Berry. The type is ITC
Galliard, designed by Matthew Carter in 1978. Galliard is based on the
16th-century French humanist typefaces of Robert Granjon, although it is
not a direct revival, and this version was digitized by Matthew Carter in
1992 for Carter & Cone Type Inc. *Printed by Bang Printing.*